SOUTHWEST INDIAN COOKBOOK

SOUTHWEST INDIAN COOKBOOK

by MARCIA KEEGAN

CLEAR
LIGHT PUBLISHERS

To my Pueblo and Navajo friends with love

Copyright © 1987 by Marcia Keegan
Fourth Printing, 1990
Clear Light Publishers

Clear Light Publishers
823 Don Diego
Santa Fe, New Mexico 87501

International Standard Book
Number 940666-03-0
Library of Congress Catalog Card
Number 77-84927

Printed and bound in Hong Kong by
Book Art Inc., Toronto

ACKNOWLEDGEMENTS

The idea for this book evolved out of my 20 years immersion as a photojournalist in Pueblo & Navajo cultures.

I shared many meals with my friends in the southwest and grew to love their food. Sorry that the rest of the world was missing out on this experience, I asked for written recipes. There were none.

It has taken much work on the part of many of my friends to refine family tradition and history into cups and tablespoons and I want to thank those who helped me in this endeavor.

I want to especially thank: Agnes Dill, Paul Enciso, Trina Enciso, Julia Roybal, Isadora Sarracino, Louva Dahozy, Katherine De Arvisa, Rosemary Cordova, Veronica Chapman, Ramalda Shattuck, Clara Leon, Bim Marcus, Leandra Bernal, Josephine Bernal, Reyesita Bernal, Sam Day III, Shirley Day, Richard Martinez, Lucy Martinez, and Maria Bebout.

I also want to thank Ellen Resch, Letta and Keith Wofford, Mary Keegan, Harmon Houghton, Kay De and Dan Fullerton, Howard Bryan and Stacy Pearl from Montana Palace for testing the recipes.

A special thanks to Maria Carvainis and Jane Butel from Pecos Valley Spice Co. who were of great help in editing and solidifying the recipes.

I want to thank Pablita Velarde for writing the foreword and for her creative inspiration through the years.

Marcia Keegan

LIST OF RECIPES

SOUPS AND APPETIZERS

Summer squash soup	40
Zuñi corn soup	40
Piñon soup	41
Piñon and mint soup	41
Pinto bean soup	42
Black bean soup	42
Potato and tomato cream soup	43
Lamb soup	43
Corn salad	44
Bean salad	44
Guacomole I	45
Guacomole II	45
Guacomole III	46
Red Chili sauce	47
Green Chili sauce	47
San Ildefonso salsa	47
Salsa	47

VEGETABLE DISHES

Cracked chicos	60
Corn with pinto beans	60
Chicos with pinto beans	61
Pinto beans	61
Baked corn and zucchini	62
Zuñi succotash	62
Green tomato stew	63
Skillet squash	63
Chili squash	64
Corn tortilla casserole	64
Corn and pumpkin stew	65
Baked pumpkin	65
Corn dumplings	66
Egg dumplings	66
Green chili fry	67
Chili stew	67
Green chili stew	68
Calabacitas	68
Fried cabbage stew	69
Stuffed sweet peppers	69
Garbanzo stew	70
Posole	70
Hopi corn stew with blue cornmeal dumplings	71
Blue cornmeal dumplings	71

MEAT DISHES

Juniper lamb stew	84
Mutton stew	84
Taos rabbit	85
Pueblo venison stew	85
Venison steak	86
Chili venison	86
Tamales	87
Feast day pork roast	88
Chili pork	88
Green chili with pork	89
Popcorn ox tails stew	89
Barbecue pork	90
Navajo stew with corn dumplings	91
Corn dumplings	91
Lamb, corn, and tomato stew with dumplings	92
Dumplings	92
Indian mish-mash	93
Beef stew with green chilies	93
Burrito	94
Meat jerky	94
Pueblo fish fry	95
Taos Pueblo fish fry	95

BREADS AND DESSERTS

Indian fry bread	107
Pueblo bread	108
Navajo kneel down bread	108
Sopapillias	109
Tortillas	109
Wild sage bread	110
Blue corn bread	110
Frying pan corn bread	111
Sweet pumpkin bread	111
Pueblo corn pudding	112
Pueblo peach crisp	112
Little fruit pies	113
Pueblo Indian cookies	113
Blue cornmeal cakes	114
Navajo cake	114
Piñon cakes	115
Pocket book rolls	115
Indian bread pudding	116
Taos pudding	116
Easter pudding	117
Date pudding	117
Apricot rice pudding	118
Fry bread pudding	118
Pueblo turnovers	119
Laguna cake pudding	119
Piñon cookies	120
Feast day cookies	120

I have known Marcia Keegan for many years and I am really happy and proud that I am her friend. I think readers will find her cookbook very special, not only because Marcia is such a wonderful photographer, but also because her interest in the Indian people is deep and sincere, as human being to human being. She has spent many years collecting these recipes and has enjoyed many of them in our homes. And she understands that food has deep spiritual significance for the Indian people.

Before we eat whatever we grow, we feed the Spirit World. We have to let them have the first taste to express our gratitude. And for every meal that we eat after that, we have to feed the Spirit World first, and then we eat. Sometimes we forget, but then the old-timers remind us, because they always set the example at the table. They take a little pinch of the food and throw it to the four winds—so that the Spirit World will have the same food that we are having here on earth. And since the Spirits help to raise the food, it possesses great powers to heal the body and mind.

Sometimes corn pollen is used for medicine, and it's also used in ceremonial dances as a body paint, and blue corn meal especially they say is very good for aches in the joints. If you make a little paste of it with some warm water, and just rub that on aching joints, it's supposed to take the aches away. I've never had that many aches and I've never had to use it, so I'm not sure. But the old people used to use it like that. And others sliced wild potatoes if they had a real bad headache; they used to paste the slices around their foreheads, and tie a handkerchief over it to cure the headache. And all kinds of roots that grow wild are used for medicines, and to help us have a healthy life.

I think Marcia's photographs of the foods are very special for people to see and the recipes are tasty to prepare and serve. Many of our main foods are included in this cookbook—among them, chili, beans, stews and breads—lots of breads. We have several different kinds of bread that we can make either from wheat flour or corn flour. Some of these corn flour breads are the blue corn-meal muffins, and the blue corn-meal cake, and the *atoles*. Chiles, of course, can be eaten raw, either red or green, or made into stew or relish or paste. Chili paste is delicious on a nice big slice of Indian bread or on a fresh tortilla—a white tortilla cooked on the stove, or on fry bread. You can use chili paste on all kinds of bread and have a nice snack.

I think readers will enjoy this book for its recipes, it thoughts, and its beauty.

Pablita Velarde
Santa Clara Pueblo

INTRODUCTION

Many of the foods that we now enjoy and take for granted are American Indian in origin. Until the discovery of the Americas the rest of the world knew nothing about such foods as corn, squash, melons, gourds, pumpkins, beans, and chili peppers—crops which were coaxed from an arid land centuries before Columbus, and which are still cultivated today.

The Pueblos and Navajos are accomplished cooks who prepare food by instinct and consider cooking an art that cannot be restricted by measuring cups. Many of their favorite dishes are familiar to all of us... chili, bean soups, bread puddings, and barbecue sauces. Others are exotic and intriguing... posole, piñon cake, and Navajo kneel down bread. Since Pueblos and Navajos prepare foods from "a pinch of this and a palm full of that," I have worked hard with my Indian friends and food editor Maria Carvainis to standardize the recipes in this cookbook so they can be prepared in any kitchen. I have also included here as well their personal statements about the significance of foods in legends, ceremony, and in their daily lives.

These recipes and statements are representative of the nineteen Indian Pueblos in New Mexico and the vast Navajo nation in northern Arizona.

Among the Pueblos and Navajos each meal is preceded by a prayer. The American Indian regards food as a precious gift and so treats it with reverence.

According to a Zuñi creation myth, Sun Father is the mate of Mother Earth. Their children are both the animals and the crops.

The sacred nature of food is everywhere evident in Indian culture. The dances, prayers and ceremonies all reflect the significance and value of food in daily existence. Buffalo, Deer, Bean, Turtle, Eagle, Corn and Evergreen dances have been an integral part of Indian ceremonies for centuries. And when food is taken, a little is always given back—either to the fire or to the earth—in order to replenish the source in a symbolic gesture of thanks.

Food is a source of healing as well as nourishment in the Southwest. Corn pollen is placed in a Navajo sand painting to cure the sick and special herbs have been used as medicines for centuries.

According to Zuñi belief...

> *"Five things alone are necessary to the sustenance and*
> *comfort of the Indians among the children of the earth.*
> *The sun, who is the Father of all*
> *The earth, who is the Mother of men,*
> *The water, who is the Grandfather,*
> *The fire, who is the Grandmother,*
> *Our brothers and sisters the Corn and seeds of growing things."*

Other special songs are sung as the seeds are planted and all who have experienced a traditional Indian dance know the intimacy, harmony and intangible bond between Mother Earth and her children.

The spiritual and ceremonial roles of food in the Southwest, its healing and nourishing powers, are presented in this book along with native recipes.

According to a Zuñi Pueblo chant:

> *"Watch well o'er your seed—things and children!*
> *Speak wisely to these our new children!*
> *Henceforth they shall be your first speakers,*
> *And the peace-making shields of your people."*

Marcia Keegan

PROLOGUE

The following is a dialogue between Agnes Dill of Isletta Pueblo, prominent Indian woman leader and Paul Enciso, Taos Pueblo (& Apache) who is a well-known artist and craftsman.

PAUL   Anciently and traditionally, what is important to the Pueblos is the sacredness of the food which they eat. So the food must be carefully prepared and washed, and a lot of care goes into the making. Because of the sacredness of the food itself, cooking is just like handling any craft. If you're making a kachina doll, or any kind of thing like this— moccasin making, or pottery—you never measure anything. And in the same way, you just have a certain kind of feel that you get even for food. And when you prepare it, you just put in as much as you feel is right. And I know my grandmother used to say, "If you're doing the right things, if you have that spark of faith in you,"—and when I'm speaking of faith, I'm speaking of everything that surrounds the life of the person— "...because of that, you can never make a mistake." And then you put in just so much off the palm of your hand, and that's enough. That's right. And you don't need another kind of measurement.

AGNES   It depends on how much you're making, how much you're cooking. If you're cooking for a small family, then you say, well, this is about right. But if you're cooking for a big family, then you say, well, this is about right. You use a lot more, and you just measure in your hand to see how much—say if you're making a big potful of soup, maybe two gallons or three gallons. And you put a big pinch of salt in the palm of your hand—the Indians always used the ground salt, their own Indian salt from the salt lakes, and they used to grind it. And a lot of times they would just take a pinch and put it in. So preparing food is like a craft, like painting a picture, or making a pot. There's a feeling that really goes into it—anything that is made by hand—to an Indian that is.

For instance, whenever corn is being ground, there are certain things that go with it, and so the woman never tires out in grinding corn. She can grind it for three or four hours straight, because while she grinds, the men come and sing. And in the grinding songs they tell you almost what to do. And you have to grind to the beat, to the rhythm of the songs. You have your *metatel*, or your four grinding stones in degrees of coarseness and fineness. The first one is a coarse one, then the next one, and the next one is the very finest. And the women are all sitting in back of these. Usually my grandmother or my aunt was the one who "broke up"—that's the cracking of the corn. Then the corn was handed over to the next stone. And then we ground it. And in the singing, it tells you to keep grinding, and you grind in rhythm. It's a beautiful song. I think it's all in Laguna.
PAUL   The grinding song may tell you first of all that what you're handling is very sacred, and that you've got to put yourself in tune with that spirit of what you're doing, so it doesn't become a chore to you, but it becomes part of you. You're creating something, you're doing something. And what you must do is master it, so that as you begin, and the

rhythm begins to flow through you, you just begin that feeling, and after you're through with grinding, then the feeling goes on to the person at the next stone, who grinds the corn down a little bit more, and a little bit more. And a lot of times stories are told that remind you of life itself, how you must go through life, how you must walk, just like the corn has come up from the stalk, and also be thankful, not only to Mother Earth and to Father Sky, and also to the sun for what it provides, but also to the Creator of All for creating these things. He has prepared the corn for us to one stage, and now we prepare it in different stages for our own use. And this is why we must be thankful. Because eventually what comes from the ground goes back to the ground, and we just keep exchanging, and so the grinding song tells the entire story, and so it shows our gratefulness for all this, the cycle. The cycle is never broken. It's an eternal thing, and the grinding song makes us a part of it.
AGNES   And corn is a very sacred food, because in the legends, when the corn finally comes up, the corn becomes a man. Corn comes from the earth—it's a thing that's been given to us by the Great Spirit. So the corn is used in sacred ceremonies and is universal throughout the whole Indian nation.

A translation of a Taos Pueblo corn grinding song by Paul Enciso

"From the corn we gather the pollen. The pollen that is like gold, reminds us of the color of anointment of the ancient ones. Grinding the corn it reminds us of heaven and it reminds us of earth. It reminds us that Father Sky and Mother Earth will unite forever.

"From the corn we learn to live, we learn the life that is ours, by grinding the corn we learn the footsteps of life. We go through a purification, until we are like dust. The corn came from the dust, from Mother Earth, and it gives life, like from Father Sky.

"We are like the kernel that comes from the corn. With it we bring life, like the seed of the corn. Corn is the fruit of the gods, it was brought to us by the creator, that we may remember him. Our lives, we must remember that they are holy. The corn is sacred. We are sacred. We hold the seeds of the gods to the future."

Navajo girl scattering corn meal as a prayer at sunrise

Corn is the principal Pueblo food. The Pueblos traditionally believe their bodies are basically composed
of corn and that as a result they share with the grain
a simple essence. Corn is planted in the spring, and
harvested in the late fall.

The tasks of the corn harvest are carried out by
nearly the whole population of the villages, and the season
is one of happiness and festivity.

The corn dance in which both men and women participate is a prayer that there may be plenty of rain for the growing corn and that there may be a bountiful harvest. The women wear on their heads turkey feathers and prayer plumes. Both men and women carry evergreen branches and corn in their hands. The men carry hollow gourd rattles containing pebbles which they shake to simulate falling rain.

So they dance from sunrise to sunset to bring rain, while nearby men sing ancient chants while they beat a large drum to imitate the thunder.

Corn Dance at San Juan Pueblo

Santa Clara corn dancer

Sandia Pueblo man cultivating field

San Juan Pueblo farmer gathering muskmelons

Indian corn and gourds

When tiny g[...]
of corn pollen are plac[...]
a sand painting, that [...]
ing acquires healing po[...]
It will be created for s[...]
one who is ill so that p[...]
will recover and be in[...]
mony again with all [...]
things.

Navajo sheep[...]

n Pueblo woman
ng corn

During a Navajo wedding, the grandmother of the bride presents the newly married couple with a special basket filled with cornmeal. The bride and groom exchange a pinch of the golden substance with one another. The tradition is an ancient one.

The Shattuck sisters sampling their cooking at Isleta Pueblo.

An Indian Pueblo dinner of red chili, green chili stew and bread baked in an horno or outdoor oven.

A variety of Indian foods against a backdrop of the
Sandia (watermelon) mountains in New Mexico.

There in the west
 is the home of the raingods,
There in the west
 is their water pool,
In the middle of the water pool
 is the spruce tree
 that they use as a ladder,
Up from the water the raingods
 draw the crops which give us life,
East from there, on the place
 where we dance, they lay the crops,
Then up from that place the people
 receive crops and life

         Acoma Pueblo chant

"Each time a woman would cook anything, she would put some of it back in the fire and pray. 'May we be taken care of good today and may my family live well and happy'—a prayer like that. And when she made corn meal mush she would stir it with a stick and she would say a prayer for more rain. 'Today, may we have more rain so we'll have better crops, and may my family have good health.' The women would say a prayer before each meal and then the men would say one after the meal. Indian people are very prayerful people. Here's one of our prayers:"

> *May my children have all things to eat*
> *and be happy;*
> *May the people of the outlying villages*
> *all laugh and be happy;*
> *May the growing children all have things to*
> *eat and be happy;*
> *May we have all kinds of seeds and all things*
> *good;*
> *May we inhale the sacred breath of life;*
> *May our fathers and our mothers bring us*
> *happy days."*

Louva Dahozy
Navajo

"When we were children we didn't have any popcorn or anything like that, so they used to roast the blue corn in the ovens, the ovens they make bread in. I must have been maybe eight or nine years old. Because we used to look forward to the time when they'd roast the corn in the oven. And they'd leave the corn overnight. You know, they'd husk the corn, and they'd let it dry, and after it's dry they'd take it off the cob, and then they'd put it out to dry, and then they'd put it in the oven one whole night. After they were finished maybe making bread or something like that, when the oven would be just warm enough to put your corn in. It would be overnight.

"And they used to roast it in there, and after we'd take it out we used to be so happy, because we didn't have anything like popcorn or anything, and we used to eat it just like popcorn. And I think that was our most enjoyable time, the time in early autumn, when they used to roast the corn, and we'd look forward to having that corn roasted so we could eat it like popcorn. And today they still eat it and it's called parched corn."

Julia Roybal
San Ildefonso Pueblo

"When I was a little girl, we used to hunt for wild food, like wild spinach, and wild celery, and wild onions, and all of these things. We took gunnysacks and picked wild spinach—we called it 'fashue'—and sort of dried it. My mother dried it in the summertime, and we had that for winter. Also wild turnips, which we dried. All of those things are part of the native foods.

"And I also remember when I was a little girl, early in the morning, my mother would wake me up and say, before sunup, 'go distant and say a prayer.' And then I'd take white corn meal, already ground, and pray for myself and for my home, always to the east. Then at noontime, when I would come back from herding sheep, I would take corn pollen again and I'd go distant and say a prayer again. And then in the evening before the sun was down, I'd go distant and use yellow corn meal and would pray again. But I would never pray on the north side. I think it was because that's where the evil is, everything bad was on the north side. I would pray every day. That was our way.

"There are six colors of corn: yellow, white, blue, black, red and speckled. And each color stands for a direction: North, south, east and west, up and down. The solid colors are for the four main directions. White is for the east, where the sun rises, and the blue is for the west. Yellow is for the North and Red is for the South.

"In a ceremony, when they're about to blow tobacco smoke and incense to the six directions, they sing the song of corn and growth."

Agnes Dill
Isleta Pueblo

Ha-'o, my mother, ha-o, my mother,
Due west, blue corn ear, my mother,
Due eastward, blooming blue-bird flower,
Decorate our faces, bless us with flowers.
Thus being face-decorated,
Being blessed with flowers,
We shall be delighted, we shall be delighted.
Ha-o, my mother, ha-o, my mother.

Due east, white corn ear, my mother,
Due westward, blooming butterfly flower,
Decorate our faces, bless us with flowers.
Thus being face-decorated,
Being blessed with flowers,
We shall be delighted, we shall be delighted.
Ha-o, my mother, ha-o, my mother.

Due south, red corn ear,
Due northward, blooming maiden blossom,
Decorate our faces, bless us with flowers.
Thus being face-decorated,
Blessed with flowers,
We shall be delighted, we shall be delighted.
Ha-o, my mother, ha-o, my mother.

Due above, black corn ear, my mother.
Due downward, blooming sunflower,
Decorate our faces, bless us with flowers.
Thus being face-decorated,
Being blessed with flowers,
We shall be delighted, we shall be delighted.
Ha-o, my mother, ha-o, my mother.

Due below, sweet corn ear, my mother.
Due upward, blooming, all kinds of flowers.
Decorate our faces, bless them with flowers.
Thus being face-decorated,
Being blessed with flowers,
We shall be delighted, we shall be delighted.
Ha-o, my mother, ha-o, my mother.

Zuñi Pueblo chant

"I come from a very large family, very large—my mother raised 17 children. Fifteen of her own and two more. One of the things she used to say is, 'follow the cows, and whatever the cows eat, you bring back.' We knew that the animals knew what was good to eat, and that's what we'd bring back. And this is one of the things that we were happy for. The animals knowing instinctively and by nature what was good for them to eat, well, we knew that that would be good for us as well."

Paul Enciso
Taos Pueblo & Apache

SUMMER SQUASH SOUP

4 medium-sized summer squash, cubed
1 clove garlic, minced
1 onion, chopped
1 teaspoon ground red chili
½ teaspoon oregano
6 tablespoons butter or other shortening
1½ cups chicken bouillon
½ cup milk

In a heavy skillet, saute squash over low heat with seasonings in butter until squash is tender.

Place mixture in blender and add broth. Puree and place in a heavy saucepan.

Add milk and gently simmer for 5 minutes.

Yield: 6 servings

ZUÑI CORN SOUP

1 medium-sized onion, sliced thinly
1 tablespoon butter or oil
2 cups lamb, diced
6 cups water or beef bouillon
2 cups dried posole corn*
1 teaspoon salt
1 teaspoon ground red chili

Saute onion in butter or oil in a large heavy saucepan, until onion is slightly wilted. Add lamb and 3 cups of water or bouillon and simmer until tender for about 1½-2 hours.

Add corn, along with remaining ingredients, and simmer until corn is tender.

*If posole corn is not available, canned hominy can be used as a substitute—add hominy to soup for the last 15-20 minutes of cooking-time.

Yield: 6 servings

PIÑON SOUP

1   pound raw piñon nuts
1   quart milk
2   cups chicken bouillon
5   scallions, sliced
2   coriander seeds
1   teaspoon dried mint, crushed
¼   teaspoon pepper
Minced chives to garnish

Heat all ingredients except chives in a large heavy saucepan until mixture simmers. Simmer for 20-30 minutes.

Puree mixture in a blender until smooth. Reheat and serve garnished with chives or serve iced.

Note: Small portions of the soup should be served as the soup is very rich.

Yield: 6 servings

PIÑON AND MINT SOUP

1   lamb or beef bone with meat
6   cups water
¾   cup piñon nuts, shelled and
    coarsely chopped
3   cups cooked chick peas, drained
1   onion, thinly sliced
1   teaspoon dried mint

In a large heavy saucepan, cook soup bone in water for 1 hour or longer. Remove meat from bone.

Add remaining ingredients and simmer for 15 minutes.

Remove soup from heat and add mint.

Yield: 6 servings

PINTO BEAN SOUP

1   lamb bone, cracked
1   medium-sized onion, chopped
1   teaspoon salt
4   peppercorns, crushed
1   teaspoon crushed coriander
1   clove garlic, minced
2   cups dry pinto beans, cleaned and rinsed
3½ quarts water

In a large heavy saucepan, place all the ingredients. Bring mixture to a boil and reduce heat to low. Simmer covered for 4 hours or until beans are tender, adding water as needed.

Remove bone from pan. (The lamb will fall away from the bone in cooking.) Serve hot.

Yield: 8 servings

BLACK BEAN SOUP

2   cups dry black beans (2 lb cans)
1   cup minced onion
¼   cup oil
2   cloves garlic, peeled and mashed
1   cup water
2   teaspoon salt
1   teaspoon ground red chili

Boil beans until tender. Saute onion in oil in a large heavy saucepan until onion is slightly wilted. Add garlic and 2 cups beans with liquid. Mash beans with fork.

Add remaining beans with liquid. Add water, salt, and chili. Simmer, covered, for 40 minutes, stirring occasionally.

Yield: 6 servings

POTATO AND TOMATO CREAM SOUP

2½ cups potatoes, diced
3   cups tomatoes, peeled, seeded, and cubed
2   onions, sliced
1½ teaspoons flour
2   tablespoons lard or other shortening
3   green chiles, diced (4 ounce can)
2   tablespoons ground red chili
½   cup light cream

Bring potatoes, tomatoes, and onions to a boil in 1 quart of water. Reduce heat to low and simmer for an hour.

Mix flour and lard, add green chilies, and stir into potato-tomato mixture. Stir in red chili blending thoroughly. Simmer for 20 minutes.

Add cream and simmer 5 minutes longer.

Yield: 6 servings

LAMB SOUP

1 lamb bone with meat
6 cups water
1 cup green beans, sliced
1 cup green peas
1 onion, sliced
1 medium-sized green pepper, cored and diced
2 cloves garlic, minced
2 teaspoons oregano
1 small can of green chilies, chopped
2 teaspoons salt

Cook soup bone in water in a large heavy saucepan for 1 hour or longer. Remove meat form bone.

Add remaining ingredients and simmer for 30 minutes. Add salt, stir, and serve.

Yield: 6 servings

CORN SALAD

3   cups cooked fresh or frozen corn
    kernels
½   cup pimento, sliced thinly
1   cup cooked lima beans
¾   cup chopped onion
1½ cups green pepper, finely chopped
1   teaspoon salt
1   teaspoon ground red chili
¼   cup vinegar
⅓   cup oil

Combine corn, pimento, lima beans,
onion, and green pepper in a large
mixing bowl.

Combine salt, chili, and
vinegar in another bowl. Slowly pour
in oil, beating constantly.

Pour dressing over corn mixture and
toss thoroughly. Allow salad to
marinate, covered, for at least 2 hours
in the refrigerator before serving.

Yield: 6 servings

BEAN SALAD

2   cups cooked pinto beans
2   cups cooked green beans
1   large onion, peeled and sliced thinly
2   cloves garlic, peeled and mashed
1   large sweet pepper, seeded and
    sliced thinly
½   cup sugar
1   teaspoon ground red chili
2   teaspoons salt
⅓   cup vinegar
½   cup oil

Combine pinto and green beans,
onion, garlic, and pepper in a large
bowl.

Combine sugar, chili, salt, and
vinegar in another bowl. Slowly pour
in oil, beating constantly.

Pour over beans and toss thoroughly.
Allow beans to marinate, covered, for
at least 2 hours in the refrigerator
before serving.

Yield: 6-8 servings

GUACAMOLE I

1 large ripe avocado, peeled and
   pitted
1 onion, peeled and minced
1 clove garlic, peeled and minced
2 tomatoes, peeled and diced
1 fresh hot green chili pepper,
   chopped, or 1 teaspoon crushed red
   chili
Juice of one lemon or lime
Salt to taste

In a mixing bowl, cube the avocado
with two knives.

Add remaining ingredients. Mix
thoroughly. Serve immediately or
chill, covered, for at least 1 hour
before serving. Serve with tostados.

Yield: 6 servings

GUACAMOLE II

1 large ripe avocado, peeled and
   pitted
1 onion, peeled and minced
1 clove garlic, peeled and minced
2 tomatoes, peeled, seeded and diced
Juice of 1 lemon or lime
¼ teaspoon coriander
¼ teaspoon salt
Freshly ground pepper to taste
¼ cup finely chopped piñon nuts

Puree the avocado in a blender or put
through a food mill.

Combine remaining ingredients,
except for the piñon nuts, and add
pureed avocado.

Chill, covered, for at least 1 hour
before serving. Serve garnished with
piñon nuts.

Yield: 6 servings

RED CHILI SAUCE

2 tablespoons lard or bacon drippings
2 tablespoons flour
¼ cup ground red chili (mild or hot)
1 fresh garlic clove, minced
  Pinch each of Mexican oregano
  and cumin
2 cups water
¾ teaspoon salt

Add the flour to melted lard at low heat. Add the chili, starting with the smaller quantity, adding more after the water is well mixed into the paste. Stir constantly when adding the water continuing to stir until a smooth sauce is obtained. Simmer for about 15 minutes. Salt to taste.

GREEN CHILI SAUCE

2 small onions, chopped
2 large tomatoes, peeled, seeded,
  and chopped
6 garlic cloves, peeled and mashed
4 green chili peppers, roasted,*
  peeled, and diced
4 tablespoons tomato paste
2 teaspoons salt
1 teaspoon coriander
¼ teaspoon crushed red hot pepper

Puree all the ingredients in a blender.

Cook the puree in 4 tablespoons of oil for 5 minutes or until sauce has thickened.

*To roast chili peppers, place peppers on a baking tin in a moderate oven for about 25 minutes or until browned on all sides.

Yield: 4 servings

SAN ILDEFONSO SALSA

3 strips bacon, cut into thin strips
2 medium-sized yellow onions,
   peeled and minced
3 small hot green chili peppers,
   minced
2 cups canned tomatoes
½ teaspoon crushed cumin seed
1 teaspoon sugar
1 teaspoon salt
1 clove garlic, peeled and minced
Juice of ½ a lemon or lime
2 dashes Tabasco
1 cup grated sharp Cheddar cheese

Brown the bacon in a large heavy
skillet.

Add onion and saute until slightly
wilted.

Mix in the peppers and tomatoes and
simmer, stirring for 15 minutes.

Remove from heat and stir in
remaining ingredients. Garnish with
cheese and serve. Use tortilla chips for
dipping.

Yield: 4 servings

SALSA

1 cup onion
2 garlic cloves
1 cup of diced tomatoes
1 cup green or red chili
   (can use 4 ounce can of green chili)
½ teaspoon salt
1 tablespoon ground red chili

Simmer all ingredients, add salt to
taste. Allow to marinate at least 15
minutes. Can be used as chili relish.

Delicious piñon nuts, gathered from the many piñon trees in the land of the Pueblos and Navajos.

Place unshelled piñon nuts in a large baking pan and roast at 300 degrees for one hour stirring frequently so that the nuts become evenly browned. No oil is needed since they have natural oil.

Early winter is "quiet season" at Taos Pueblo,
a time that ancient custom and the orders of the
Pueblo Council reserve "to let the earth rest."

Posole, a mixture of hominy, meat and chili, is a
traditional corn dish served throughout the year at
the pueblo.

Red chili in early snow

Taos woman and child

Red chili is harvested in the early autumn and dried in the sun. The dry chili peppers are washed and the stems, seeds and white veins are removed unless seeds are retained for hot chili. The pods are then usually made into a pulp fresh for each use.

Green chili peppers are harvested just before they turn color and are used fresh and roasted. Roasted green chili peppers, skinned, split and seeded, are used as a topping for fried eggs, hamburgers and grilled meats. They are an important ingredient in soups, stews, casseroles and many other Indian dishes.

Corn, beans, squashes, pumpkin and chilies predominate in Pueblo and Navajo cooking.

Visiting a pueblo today, one will find red chili peppers, strings of beans, and corn, all in the sun to dry. There will be gourds and garlic, squash and onion, corn and watermelons.

"Lots of Indian foods that we used to have a long time ago, we still have today and still can use. Squash, melons, muskmelons and especially corn. We prepare corn about 250 different ways. One way is Navajo cake, baked in the ground. Other ways are corn mush, pancakes, corn breads and paper breads. When we plant corn, squash, melon, anything, we say a prayer. Often we ask for rain because we don't have any irrigation water on the reservation. Every time we say a prayer we ask for water. We ask for it and say thank you. The Indian people are very prayerful and sincere about their food in the prayers. According to a Navajo chant."

Truly in the East
The white bean
And the great corn-plant
Are tied with the white lightning.
Listen! rain approaches!
The voice of the bluebird is heard.
Truly in the East
The white bean
And the great squash
Are tied with the rainbow.

Louva Dahozy
Navajo

"Navajos are always sharing food. They share it with other people who live around them. We're related by clans. We all have clans and clan members all live at one place. You know each other's life. Foods are used differently in different clans. We're the banana clan. It doesn't mean we eat bananas. Way back, I don't know when, my relatives probably lived where there were bananas. People who lived around water are the water clan. We do still use wild banana in our foods, even today. We can prepare wild banana lots of ways—cook it and eat it like sugar. It's the only thing sweet within our foods.

"In the Navajo way, when we're introduced to another Navajo, we have to say your name and clan. And we're not supposed to marry within our own clan, but from another clan because we're related. I have a son, people ask him what clan are you, he says I'm banana-split clan. Wild banana are shaped like egg plant, and you can get them in September. Yucca banana is the wild banana. If you don't cook it, it tastes like soap. But if you cook it, it's just like sugar beet and it tastes really good. And you dry it and use it in winter time."

Louva Dahozy
Navajo

CRACKED CHICOS

1½ cups dry corn kernels
1   cup fresh chili sauce or ¼ cup ground chili
2   tablespoons lard or cooking oil
1   small onion, chopped
1   clove garlic, peeled and mashed
1½ teaspoons salt

Crack dry corn in a food grinder or place kernels in a plastic bag and crack with a rolling pin.

Cook corn in water to cover for 1 hour or until tender. Drain water from pan and reserve.

Saute onion in lard or oil. Add garlic, corn, chili sauce or powder, and salt. Stir in water form corn and simmer until mixture thickens.

Yield: 4 servings

CORN WITH PINTO BEANS

1   cup dry pinto beans
2   cups frozen corn kernels
½   pound salt pork, diced
1   medium-sized onion, chopped
1   tablespoon lard or oil

In a large heavy saucepan, place pinto beans, corn, and salt pork in water to cover and bring to a boil. Simmer for 2 hours or until tender.

Saute onion in lard or oil. Add to beans and corn mixture and serve.

Yield: 6 servings

CHICOS WITH PINTO BEANS

1 cup dry pinto beans
1 cup chicos (dry corn kernels)
½ pound salt pork, diced
1 medium-size onion, chopped
1 tablespoon lard or oil

Clean and rinse pinto beans and chicos.

In a large heavy saucepan place pinto beans, chicos, and salt pork in water to cover and bring to a boil. Simmer for 4 hours or until tender.

Saute onion in lard or oil. Add to beans and chico mixture and serve.

Yield: 6 servings

PINTO BEANS

3 cups dry pinto beans
6 cups water
1 large onion, thinly sliced
1 cup cooked ham, diced
Oil or other shortening

Clean and wash pinto beans and soak overnight.

Cook beans in water with salt for 3 hours, or until tender.

Saute onion in lard and add ham. Add mixture to beans and serve.

Yield: 8 servings

BAKED CORN AND ZUCCHINI

3   ears of corn or 2 cups frozen corn kernels
1   medium-sized onion, finely chopped
1   clove garlic, minced
3   tablespoons lard or oil
½   pound zucchini, scrubbed and cubed ¼-inch thick
1   green pepper, sliced thinly
1½ cups peeled and chopped tomatoes
1½ teaspoons ground red chili
Salt and pepper to taste
½   cup shredded Longhorn cheese

If using fresh corn, scrape off kernels from cob with a sharp knife.

In a heavy skillet, saute onion and garlic in lard or oil until onion is slightly wilted. Add zucchini and pepper and saute 3 minutes more. Add corn, tomatoes, chili powder, salt, and pepper to taste.

Pour mixture into a buttered casserole dish and bake, covered with foil, in a preheated 350° oven for 15 minutes.

Remove from oven and top with cheese. Bake another 10 minutes or until cheese is melted.

Yield: 4 servings

ZUÑI SUCCOTASH

3   cups canned pinto beans, drained
1½ cups fresh or frozen corn kernels
1½ cups fresh string beans, chopped
1½ cups water
4   tablespoons butter or shortening
1   teaspoon sugar
1   teaspoon salt
Pepper to taste
2   tablespoons shelled sunflower seeds, crushed

In a large heavy saucepan, place all the ingredients, except for the sunflower seeds, in water with 2 tablespoons butter. Simmer for 15 minutes or until vegetables are tender.

Add sunflower seeds and remaining butter and continue to simmer until mixture thickens.

Yield: 6 servings

GREEN TOMATO STEW

1½ pounds stewing beef, cut into 1-inch cubes
Flour
2 tablespoons lard or oil
1 medium-sized onion, chopped
1 clove garlic, minced
1 4-ounce can of green chili peppers, sliced
4 medium-sized green tomatoes, sliced
2 cups fresh or frozen corn kernels
2 teaspoons salt
1 teaspoon dried mint
3 cups water or beef bouillon
2 large squash or zucchini, cubed

Dredge beef in flour.

In a large heavy saucepan, brown meat slowly on all sides in lard or oil. Transfer to a plate.

Saute onion, garlic, and chili peppers in same pan until onion is slightly wilted.

Return meat to pan with tomatoes, corn and seasonings.

Simmer, covered, in water for 1½-2 hours or until meat is tender, stirring occasionally.

Add squash or zucchini and continue to simmer for 20 minutes more or until tender.

Yield: 6 servings

SKILLET SQUASH

1 medium onion, diced
1 tablespoon shortening or butter
1 small summer squash, cubed
1 small can tomato paste
1 small can green chilies, diced
½ cup cheddar cheese, shredded

In a heavy skillet saute onion in shortening or butter, until slightly wilted. Add squash and tomato paste and cook until squash is tender stirring constantly.

Add chilies and cook over low heat for 5-10 minutes. Sprinkle cheese over mixture and cook until cheese is melted.

Yield: 4 servings

CHILI SQUASH

3 medium-sized squash, diced
2 onions, chopped
1 clove garlic, minced
4 tablespoons butter or oil
1 cup tomato puree
1 small can tomato paste
1 sweet red pepper
1 small can green chilies, sliced
2 teaspoons ground red chili

In a large heavy skillet, saute squash, onions, and garlic over low heat in butter or oil until squash is lightly browned.

Add remaining ingredients and simmer, covered, for 30 minutes.

Yield: 6 servings

CORN TORTILLA CASSEROLE

1 pound ground beef
½ cup chopped onion
2½ cups chili sauce
½ teaspoon garlic salt
1 teaspoon oregano
1 dozen corn tortillas
¾ pound cheddar cheese, grated
1 can cream of chicken soup

In a heavy skillet saute beef and onion until onion is tender. Drain off excess fat.

Combine chili sauce with garlic salt and oregano.

Place a tortilla on the bottom of a 1½ quart greased casserole dish. Sprinkle some of the meat mixture, cheese, and chilisauce over the tortilla, layer the remaining tortillas in the same manner.

Combine chicken soup with ½ cup water and pour over casserole. Sprinkle with remaining cheese.

Bake casserole in a preheated oven at 325° for 30-45 minutes.

Yield: 4-6 servings

CORN AND PUMPKIN STEW

- 3 ears of fresh corn or 2 cups frozen corn kernels
- 1 medium-sized pumpkin, peeled and diced
- 1 cup water
- Salt to taste
- ¼ cup roasted piñon nuts, finely chopped

If using fresh corn, scrape off kernels from cob with sharp knife.

Place corn in a blender and puree or mash with a fork into pulp.

Place corn and pumpkin in a skillet with remaining ingredients and simmer for 25 minutes until tender.

Yield: 4 servings

BAKED PUMPKIN

- 1 medium-sized pumpkin, peeled and cubed
- 1 cup brown sugar
- 1 teaspoon melted butter
- Cinnamon

Place pumpkin in a baking pan and sprinkle with sugar and butter. Cover pan with foil and bake in a preheated 350° oven for 30 minutes or until tender.

Serve topped with cinnamon.

Yield: 4 servings

CORN DUMPLINGS

1 cup canned whole corn kernels, drained
1 cup flour
2 teaspoons baking powder
2 teaspoons salt
3 tablespoons cornmeal
¼ cup lard or other shortening

Mash corn well with a fork or grate in a blender.

Combine flour, baking powder, salt, and cornmeal. Cut in lard.

Add milk to form a soft but still stiff dough.

Drop mixture by the spoonfuls into stew. Cover stew and simmer for 15 minutes.

Yield: 6 servings

EGG DUMPLINGS

4 eggs, beaten
2½ tablespoons flour
Baking powder
Lard or oil

In a large mixing bowl combine eggs, flour, and a pinch of baking powder and blend thoroughly.

In a deep skillet heat lard or oil, use sufficient oil to fill skillet to a 2-inch level.

Drop egg mixture by the spoonful into the hot oil and fry until browned. Lift out with a slotted spoon.

Note: dumplings can be added to chili or other stews. Allow the dumplings to simmer in the stew for the last 15 minutes of cooking time.

Yield: 4 servings

GREEN CHILI FRY

5 green chili peppers, roasted,*
  peeled, seeded, and sliced
2 ears fresh corn or ½ cup frozen corn
  kernels
2 large tomatoes, diced
1 small onion, chopped
1 tablespoon lard or other shortening

If using fresh corn, scrape kernels from
cob with a sharp knife.

In a heavy skillet, combine all the
ingredients and saute in lard for 10-15
minutes or until mixture is soft.

*To roast chili peppers, place peppers
  on a baking tin in moderate oven for
  about 20 minutes or until browned on
  all sides.

Yield: 4 servings

CHILI STEW

2 pounds boneless stew meat, cubed
4 tablespoons ground red chili
6 small potatoes, boiled, skinned,
  cubed
  Salt to taste

In a heavy saucepan put meat and 3
cups of water, bring to a boil and
simmer for about one hour.

In a mixing bowl combine potatoes,
chili, and ½ cup water, mash to make a
smooth paste. Add 1½ cups water.

Add chili mixture to meat and continue
cooking for an additional hour or until
meat is tender. Add salt to taste.

Yield: 4 servings

GREEN CHILI STEW

1½ pounds boned lamb, cut into 1″ cubes
Flour
2 tablespoons lard or oil
½ teaspoon freshly ground pepper
3 dried juniper berries, crushed
1 medium-sized onion, peeled and chopped
2½ cups canned hominy, drained
1½ tablespoons ground red chili
½ teaspoon salt
1 clove garlic, peeled and mashed
1 teaspoon Mexican oregano
3 green chili peppers, peeled, seeded, and chopped
1 pint water

Coat lamb lightly with flour.

Brown lamb slowly on all sides in oil in a large heavy saucepan. While meat browns, add black pepper and juniper berries.

Transfer meat to a plate. Saute onion in pan until slightly wilted. Return meat to pan.

Add remaining ingredients and simmer, covered, for 1½ hours, stirring occasionally.

Yield: 6 servings

CALABACITAS

2 pounds ground beef
4 tablespoons lard or oil
1 large onion, chopped
3 potatoes, peeled and thinly sliced
1 cup squash or zucchini, cubed
2 small cans green chilies, chopped
2 tomatoes, sliced
Salt to taste

In a large heavy skillet, saute beef in lard or oil for 5 minutes.

Add remaining ingredients and simmer for 2 minutes.

Cover skillet and bake in a preheated 325° oven for 40 minutes.

Yield: 6 servings

FRIED CABBAGE STEW

1 large head of cabbage, coarsely
  shredded
1 pound beef, cubed
2 tablespoons lard
2 tablespoons water
Salt and pepper

In a heavy skillet brown meat in lard on
all sides.

Add cabbage, water, salt and pepper to
taste and simmer for about 30 minutes
or until tender.

Yield: 6 servings

STUFFED SWEET PEPPERS

4 large sweet red peppers
1 pound ground lamb
1 tablespoon butter or lard
1 small onion, chopped
1 cup raw mushrooms, coarsely
  chopped
½ teaspoon salt
½ teaspoon coriander
½ teaspoon cumin
¼ teaspoon freshly ground pepper
3 large tomatoes, peeled, and
  coarsely chopped
1 cup soft bread crumbs

Remove tops and seeds from peppers
and rinse peppers.

Saute lamb in butter in a large heavy
skillet. Add onion and mushrooms and
cook until slightly wilted.
Add remaining ingredients and
simmer, stirring occasionally, for 25
minutes. Remove from heat and allow
to cool.

Fill peppers with meat mixture. Place
peppers in a baking pan and bake in a
preheated 350° oven for 1 hour or until
the peppers are tender.

Yield: 4 servings

GARBANZO STEW

2 lbs cubed beef with soup bone
2 tablespoons lard or bacon drippings
1 cup dried tender garbanzos (chick peas)
1 onion chopped
¼ cup ground red chili
   Pinch each of Mexican oregano and cumin

Soak garbanzos overnight in water to cover. Brown beef cubes and soup bone. Stew garbanzos in pot of water adding salt. Bring to boil and then simmer until tender for about 2 hours. Saute onion in lard. Add onion, chili and seasonings to garbanzos and simmer together.

POSOLE

2 cups posole (dried corn)
6 cups water
2 pounds beef or pork ribs
¼ cup ground red chili (4 whole pods)
2 tablespoons onion, chopped
1 clove garlic, minced
2 teaspoon salt
2 teaspoons oregano

In a large heavy saucepan cook posole in water to cover until kernels pop. Do not add seasoning to water, otherwise posole will not become tender. Add meat, chili, and water to cover, bring to a boil. Cover pan and simmer until meat is tender, about 4 hours.

Yield: 6 servings

HOPI CORN STEW WITH BLUE CORN MEAL DUMPLINGS

2 pounds stewing beef, cut into 1-inch cubes
2 tablespoons lard or oil
1 medium-sized onion, chopped
1 small sweet green pepper, chopped
1 tablespoon ground red chili
4 cups frozen corn kernels
1 medium-sized pumpkin, peeled and cubed
2 tablespoons whole wheat flour
Salt to taste

In a large heavy saucepan, saute meat in lard or oil until lightly browned. Transfer meat to a plate.

Saute onion and green pepper in same pan until onion is slightly wilted.

Return meat to pan with chili powder, add enough water to cover meat, and simmer for 1½ hours.

Add corn, pumpkin, and salt to taste and simmer until tender.

Add flour mixed with 2 tablespoons of water to stew.

Add dumplings and simmer, covered, for 15 minutes.

Yield: 6 servings

BLUE CORN MEAL DUMPLINGS

2 cups ground blue corn meal
2 teaspoons baking powder
1 teaspoon salt
¼ cup lard or other shortening
¾ cup milk

Combine corn meal, baking powder, and salt.

Cut in lard or other shortening until mixture looks like meal.

Add milk to form a soft but still stiff dough.

Drop mixture by spoonfuls into stew.

Yield: 6 servings

May we be the ones whom your thoughts will

embrace,

For this, on this day

To our sun father,

We offer prayer meal.

To this end:

May you help us all to finish our roads.

Zuñi Pueblo chant

Acoma woman carrying water

Pueblo family at ceremonial dinner

PUEBLO FEAST DAY MENU
A typical dinner served to guests at
Indian Pueblo homes during Feast Day observances.

Bean Salad (p. 44)
Red Chili Stew (p. 67)
Green Chili Stew (p.68)
Posole (p. 70)
Pueblo Bread (p. 108) *or* Indian Fry Bread (p. 107)
Feast Day Cookies (p. 120)
Pueblo Bread Pudding (p. 116)
Cherry Kool-Aid and Coffee

A ceremonial dinner consisting of c
stew, fry bread and bread puddi

An Indian taco consists of an appetizing mixture of ground beef, tomatoes, cheese, onions, lettuce and chili served on traditional fry bread.

The name of this dish will vary depending on where it was made — from "Hopi Taco", "Tewa Taco" to "Navajo Taco". But since the recipe is the same, I've called it simply "Indian Taco".

Taos Pueblo man by fireplace

Chili is ground by hand in a bowl into powder
used to spice many Indian foods.

"At sunrise the dancers come down from the hills led into the village by the war priests. The buffalo comes first followed by the elk, deer, longhorn sheep and the antelopes. The women go down the road to meet them and as they pass by they sprinkle sacred cornmeal on the dancers and ask for blessings.

"Most all the pueblos have some kind of a Buffalo dance and they also have a Deer dance when only the deer participate.

"It is a thanksgiving dance thanking the spirit of the animal of which antler they are wearing and thanking them for giving us food from their flesh.

"At the end of the day of dancing, the deer and the mountain sheep, the elk and the antelopes are turned loose in the plaza and then the ladies chase them and whoever catches one takes the dancer home and they feed him and give him meat to take home to his family to show appreciation. It is an honor to catch a wild deer."

Pablita Velarde
Santa Clara Pueblo

"The hunters will usually get together the day before they're going to go on a hunt. They have dancing and songs as well, calling upon the gods to see them have a successful day, and also because they're going out to catch the food that they need. They never kill more than is necessary but always pray that they can catch enough for their wants and their supplies. Also before this dance and ceremony take place, the men that are going to go on the hunt usually prepare themselves by a four-day fast to have them become in tune with all of nature—that means even the animals, and the trees, and the ground—everything.

"After that is done, and of course it's very sacred, then they go off and by inspiration they are led to wherever there are animals. The animals usually, it is said, will know that the men will come to catch them, and there are certain animals that almost have the feeling that the men have gotten themselves into tune with nature, and somehow there's a natural communication, if I can say, a communication between man and nature, and the animals feel this communication. And there are some that will move on and others that know that they must be the sacrifice for mankind. Now man, in turn, at the point where the animal is there waiting for the kill, the man in turn will of course go and ask the God of Heaven, the Creator, to forgive him that he must take the life of this animal. In turn, he also asks the animal's forgiveness for taking his life. But also he tells the animal that he recognizes that that is why this beast was put here on earth, to supply us with our food. In turn, the kill is made, it is finished, and then after the animal is dead, the man will go there, and again, he will talk with him, saying that his spirit has left his body, and has gone into the spirit world, and again ask for his forgiveness, but also to let him know how thankful he is that he, the animal, will supply his family with the flesh and the buckskin and the bones and everything to both feed and clothe his family. And he has honorably done this, with great dignity, so that no dignity is taken from the animal, and the honor has never been demeaned from the man—from the hunter.

"And then of course after the animal comes back into the village, there is singing, everybody is rejoicing. Everybody joins into it, it isn't just a one-man, one-family affair, but it's an entire group. The entire village. And then of course no one ever takes everything that is there, but they share, even though one man has shot the deer, or has killed it through bow and arrow. It becomes a system of sharing, a united order, and whatever is needed for that family, that is all that is used, and then the rest of it is distributed among the people.

Paul Enciso
Taos Pueblo & Apache

JUNIPER LAMB STEW

2 pounds stewing lamb, cubed
1 tablespoon flour
2 tablespoons lard or oil
6 small onions, chopped
3 sweet green peppers, chopped
5 cups frozen corn kernels
1 cup canned tomatoes
½ cup celery, chopped
1½ teaspoons salt
5 dried juniper berries, crushed
2 teaspoons ground red chili
4 cups warm water

Combine seasonings with flour.
Dredge meat lightly.

Brown meat in lard or oil in a large
heavy saucepan. Transfer meat to a
plate. Saute onion and pepper in pan
until slightly wilted. Add corn to pan.

Return meat to pan, adding remaining
ingredients. Simmer, covered, for 1½
hours or until meat is tender, stirring
occasionally.

Yield: 4 servings

MUTTON STEW

3 pounds boneless mutton, cubed
1 large onion, chopped
2 cups cornkernels
5 small potatoes, diced
2 tablespoons oil
Salt and pepper to taste

In a large heavy skillet saute mutton in
oil, add remaining ingredients and
enough water to cover. Simmer for
about one hour or until meat is tender.

Yield: 6 servings

TAOS RABBIT

1 medium sized rabbit
2 tablespoons lard or oil
1 large onion, peeled and diced
2 quarts water
1 cup wine vinegar
3 teaspoons ground red chili
1 teaspoon salt
½ cup cornmeal (blue or yellow)

Cut rabbit into serving pieces. Place in a large saucepan and brown meat in lard or oil.

Add remaining ingredients and simmer, covered, for 1½ hours or until meat is tender.

Add cornmeal gradually to pan, blending thoroughly. Simmer for 10 minutes until sauce thickens.

Yield: 6 servings

PUEBLO VENISON STEW

2 pounds venison, cut into 1-inch cubes
Flour.
¼ cup lard or oil
1 large onion, chopped
2 cloves garlic, peeled and minced
1 medium-sized sweet green pepper, chopped
1 cup dry corn kernels
1 cup dry pinto beans
½ cup piñon nuts, chopped
¼ cup sunflower seeds, shelled and crushed
2 dried juniper berries, crushed
Salt and pepper to taste

Dredge venison in flour.

In a large heavy saucepan, saute venison until lightly browned. Transfer to a plate.

Saute onion, garlic and pepper in same pan until onion is slightly wilted.

Return meat to pan with remaining ingredients. Add enough water to cover venison and vegetables. Simmer for 3 hours or until tender.

Yield: 6 servings

VENISON STEAK

1 venison round steak, 1-inch thick
Flour
1 teaspoon ground red chili
Salt to taste
1 medium-sized onion, chopped
2 teaspoons lard or other shortening
3 small tomatoes
3 dried juniper berries, crushed

Dredge steak in flour, ground chili and salt.

In a large heavy skillet, saute onion in lard or shortening until slightly wilted.

Add tomatoes and berries and enough water to cover. Simmer for 50 minutes or until tender.

Note: Beef may be substituted for venison

Yield: 4 servings

CHILI VENISON

2 pounds venison meat, cut into
   1-inch cubes
Flour
¼ cup lard or other shortening
1 large onion, chopped
2 cloves garlic, peeled and minced
2 4-ounce cans of green chili peppers, sliced
4 medium-sized green tomatoes, cubed
1 teaspoon salt
1 teaspoon cumin
½ teaspoon oregano

Dredge venison in flour.

In a large heavy saucepan, saute meat in lard or other shortening until lightly browned. Transfer to a plate.

Saute onion, garlic, and chili peppers in same pan until onion is slightly wilted.

Return meat to pan with remaining ingredients. Add enough water to cover and simmer for 2-3 hours or until tender.

Yield: 6 servings

TAMALES

25 large dried corn husks
meat filling:
1½ pounds cooked shoulder pork,
   chopped
2 cloves garlic, peeled and crushed
1½ teaspoons ground red chili
¾ teaspoons cumin powder
¼ cup chili sauce, hot as desired
   Pinch of oregano
½ teaspoon tabasco sauce
1 small hot red chili pepper, crushed
1 teaspoon salt

Masa or dough
2 cups masa harina*
½ teaspoon salt
1½ cups broth from pork

*This is a special flourlike mixture used
for making tamales and tortillas. It can
be found in a specialty shop or in
Spanish groceries.

Cover the dried husks with hot water
and soak for 2 hours or until very
tender.

Boil pork in 2 cups water until it can
be shredded with a fork. Brown garlic
and pork in shortening. Make a paste
of the broth, chili, cumin powder, and
oregano and stir into the meat. Add
the remaining filling ingredients, and
simmer gently, stirring occasionally,
for about 45 minutes.

For the dough, mix the masa harina,
salt and stock together well.

To roll the tamales, spread a husk out
flat and place one tablespoon of the
masa mixture in the center and top with
a tablespoon of the meat filling. Flatten
the fillings leaving an inch at the sides
and bottom of the husk. Fold the
bottom and sides of the husk enclosing
the filling and tie securely with string.
Leave top open.

Stand the tamales, sealed end down in
a large steamer and surround them with
aluminum foil so they stand by
themselves. Fill the bottom of the
steamer with water, place a teatowel
over the top. Cover with lid and steam
the tamales for about 2½ hours.

Yield: 12 servings

FEAST DAY PORK ROAST

4 pounds pork roast
2 cups tomato puree
½ cup raisins
1 teaspoon ground red chili
½ cup chopped sweet peppers
1 tablespoon onion, chopped
1 clove garlic, mashed
1 teaspoon dried sage
1 teaspoon oregano
2 teaspoons salt
⅓ cup flour

Combine all the seasonings except for the chili powder. Rub into roast. Place roast fat side up in a baking pan and roast in a preheated 350° oven for 2½-3 hours. Reduce oven to 250°.

Pour off drippings into a skillet and add onion and green pepper and saute until slightly wilted.

Combine flour and ground chili. Add to skillet along with tomato puree and raisins and simmer for 10 minutes stirring constantly, until sauce thickens. If sauce is too thick, add a little water, gradually, until sauce reaches desired consistency.

Return roast to pan, baste with sauce, and roast for 30 minutes more, basting two or three times.

Yield: 6-8 servings

CHILI PORK

1½ pounds lean pork
Flour
1 tablespoon cooking oil
1 teaspoon salt
1½ tablespoons ground red chili
1 teaspoon oregano
1 clove garlic, peeled and mashed
3 large ripe tomatoes, peeled and diced
1 pint water

Coat pork lightly in flour.

Brown pork slowly on all sides in oil in a large heavy saucepan. While pork browns, add ground chili. Add remaining ingredients, cover, and simmer for 1½ hours, or until tender, stirring occasionally.

Yield: 6 servings

GREEN CHILI WITH PORK

2 pounds boneless pork, cut into
  1-inch cubes
Flour
6 tablespoons lard or oil
1 medium-sized onion, chopped
2 cloves garlic, peeled and minced
2 8-ounce cans of tomato sauce
2 cups canned whole corn kernels,
  drained
1 cup canned green chilies, chopped
Salt to taste
2 teaspoons oregano

Dredge pork in flour.

In a large heavy saucepan, saute pork in lard or oil until pork loses its red color. Transfer to a plate.

Saute onion and garlic in same pan until onion is slightly wilted.

Return meat to pan and add enough water to cover. Simmer for 1 hour or until meat is tender, stirring occasionally.

Add remaining ingredients and simmer for 30 minutes.

Yield: 6 servings

POPCORN OX TAILS STEW

2 pounds ox tails
½ head of small cabbage, chunked
3 sticks celery, coarsely chopped
4 medium-size carrots, diced
2 large tomatoes, coarsely diced
4 tablespoons dry or fresh coriander
4 medium-size potatoes, cubed
4 cups dry-popped popcorn

In a large pot cook ox tails in enough water to cover for 3 hours. Add water as necessary.

Remove ox tails and set aside, add all other ingredients to pot and cook for 45 minutes.

Return ox tails to soup and simmer for an additional 15 minutes.

Serve hot in bowls, sprinkled with a handful of popcorn.

Yield: 10-12 servings

BARBECUE PORK

5 pound rib roast of pork
2 medium-sized onions, peeled, and
  minced
2 cloves garlic, peeled, and minced
4 tablespoons lard or oil
3 dried juniper berries, crushed
1 teaspoon crushed coriander
1 bay leaf, crumbled
3 cups canned tomatoes
½ cup unsulfured molasses
⅔ cup cider vinegar
2 tablespoons tomato paste
1 red chili pepper, crushed
4 tablespoons ground red chili

In a large heavy saucepan, saute onion and garlic in lard or oil until onion is slightly wilted. Add juniper berries, coriander and bay leaf and saute for 5 minutes.

Add remaining ingredients and bring to a boil. Reduce heat to low and simmer for 30 minutes or until sauce is very thick.

Place roast with fat side up in a roasting pan and baste barbecue sauce over roast. Roast in a preheated 350° oven for 3 hours, basting occasionally with sauce and drippings from roast. Use remaining barbecue sauce when serving roast.

Yield: 6-8 servings

NAVAJO STEW WITH CORN DUMPLINGS

2 pound boneless lamb, cut into
   1-inch cubes
¼ cup lard or oil
1 large onion, chopped
2 cloves garlic
3 tablespoons chili powder
Salt and pepper to taste
2 cups cooked pinto beans or 1½ cup
   cooked pinto beans and ½ cup
   cooked garbanzos
3 large tomatoes, cubed
2 potatoes, peeled and diced
3 cups water

In a large heavy saucepan, saute lamb in lard or oil until lightly browned. Transfer to a plate.

Saute onion and garlic in pan until onion is slightly wilted.

Return meat to pan, adding remaining ingredients, and simmer for 2 hours or until meat is tender.

Add dumplings and simmer for 15 minutes more.

Yield: 6 servings

CORN DUMPLINGS

1 cup canned whole corn kernels,
   drained
1 cup flour
2 teaspoons baking powder
2 teaspoons salt
3 tablespoons cornmeal
¼ cup lard or other shortening

Mash corn well with a fork or grate in a blender.

Combine flour, baking powder, salt, and cornmeal. Cut in lard.

Add milk to form a soft but still stiff dough.

Drop mixture by the spoonfuls into stew.

Yield: 6 servings

LAMB, CORN, AND TOMATO STEW WITH DUMPLINGS

2 pounds boneless lamb, cut into
   1-inch cubes
¼ cup lard or oil
1 cup chopped onion
1 clove garlic, minced
4 tomatoes, peeled, seeded, and
   chopped
2 cups fresh or frozen corn kernels
¼ cup lemon juice
2 tablespoons tomato paste
1 tablespoon pure ground red chili
1 teaspoon ground coriander
Salt to taste

In a large heavy saucepan, saute lamb in lard or oil until lightly browned. Transfer to a plate.

Saute onion and garlic in the same pan until onion is slightly wilted. Return lamb to pan.

Add remaining ingredients and enough water to cover. Bring to a boil and reduce heat to low. Simmer, covered, for 1½ hours or until meat is tender.

Add dumplings and simmer for 15 minutes more.

Yield: 6 servings

DUMPLINGS

1 cup whole wheat flour
1 cup white flour
2 teaspoons baking powder
1 teaspoon salt
¼ cup lard or other shortening
¾ cup milk
2 tablespoons ground red chili
1 teaspoon salt

Combine flour, baking powder, and salt. Cut in lard or other shortening, working mixture until it looks like meal.

Add milk to form a soft but still stiff dough.

Add ground chili and mix thoroughly. (More milk, added a small amount at a time, may be necessary.)

Drop mixture by spoonfuls into stew.

Yield: 6 servings

INDIAN MISH-MASH

2 pounds ground beef
4 tablespoons lard or oil
2 medium-sized onions, chopped
4 medium-sized squash or zucchini,
    cubed
3 cups fresh or frozen corn kernels
2 4-ounce cans of green chilies, diced
1 8-ounce can of tomato sauce
Salt to taste

In a large heavy skillet, saute onion in
lard or oil until onion is slightly wilted.

Add meat and saute until lightly
browned. Add remaining ingredients
and simmer, covered, for 1 hour,
stirring occasionally.

Yield: 6 servings

BEEF STEW WITH GREEN CHILIES

2 cups chopped onion
4 slices of bacon, chopped
3 garlic cloves, minced
¼ cup lard or oil
2 pounds stewing beef, cut into 1-inch
    cubes
2 cups canned tomatoes
2 cups water or beef bouillon
2 4-ounce cans of roasted and peeled
    green chili peppers, seeded and
    sliced
1 teaspoon cumin
½ teaspoon oregano
1 teaspoon salt

In a large heavy saucepan, saute
onion, bacon and garlic in lard or oil
until onion is slightly wilted.

Add beef and brown on all sides.

Add remaining ingredients and
simmer, covered, for 2-3 hours or until
beef is tender.

Yield: 6 servings

BURRITO

2 tablespoons ground red chili
½ teaspoon Mexican oregano
½ teaspoon cumin
2 lbs. ground beef, cooked
1½ teaspoon salt
2 cups cooked pinto beans, mashed and refried
3 tablespoons onion, chopped
1 cup of grated cheddar cheese
1 teaspoon pure ground chili
½ cup of red or green chili sauce

Roll the mixture of beef, beans, onions and chili sauce in a tortilla. Place in 350° oven for 10 to 15 minutes until cheese melts. Warm chili sauce and serve over tortillas.

Yield: 4 servings

MEAT JERKY

Lean beef, venison or lamb can be used.

Slice meat into slices about ¼ inch thick. Salt moderately on both sides. Hang meat to dry in full sun, turning occasionally. At end of the day bring meat indoors and hang in a dry place. Return to full sun the following day. The meat will dry in several days to a week depending on climate and humidity. When thoroughly dried store in covered container.

PUEBLO FISH FRY

1 bonito fish, cleaned and scaled
Garlic salt
Vegetable oil

Slice bonito in bite-size pieces. Dip into garlic salt and deep-fry in hot vegetable oil. Serve with hot corn tortillas.

Note: garlic salt removes the fish smell and enhances the fish taste.

Yield: 2 servings

TAOS PUEBLO FISH BAKE

1 large trout, cleaned and scaled
1 clove of garlic, mashed
1 teaspoon red chili, powdered or crushed
1 teaspoon salt
1 teaspoon oregano
1 teaspoon onion salt
⅓ cup fresh lemon juice

Combine last six ingredients and mix thoroughly. Let stand for 15 minutes.

Marinate trout in mixture for at least 10 minutes on each side.

Wrap trout in cheese cloth, wetting the cloth with any marinade remaining, and wrap in foil.

Bake fish in preheated oven at 350° for about 1½ hours. Serve fish with hot corn tortillas.

Yield: 2 servings

The Indians are famous for their breads...flat Navajo fry bread and smooth round Pueblo bread that is baked in the horno.

The horno, the adobe outdoor oven, is of ancient origin and has been used throughout the centuries in New Mexico.

Taos Pueblo woman baking bread in horno

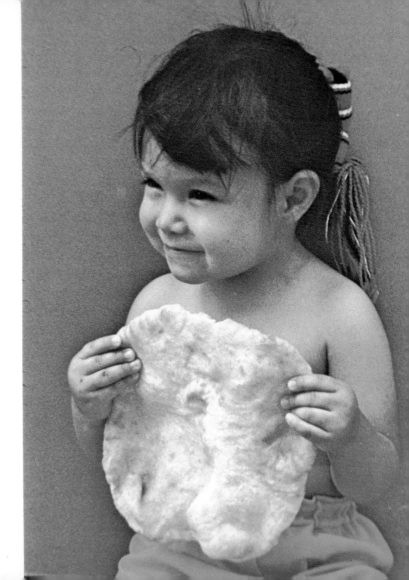

Ildefonso Pueblo woman
ing bread baked in an horno

Acoma Pueblo child eating fry bread

blo sisters
ry bread

Pudding consists
inly eggs, milk
ugar.

Tortilla is sometimes
called slap bread
because you slap it
to make it flat and round

Small Indian bread still hot as removed from horno

Hopi woman making piki bread

Ground cornmeal baked in thin translucent sheets called wafer, paper bread or piki bread. Blue cornmeal and salt are mixed with water and sage ashes so as to form a thin substance. The baker dips her fingers in this thin mixture and sweeps them across a very smooth stone, under which a fire is built.

"Making piki bread is handed down by whoever is doing the cooking—even the men, because the men cook. And each one is taught to cook when they are just little tiny things. My mother had three bake ovens for the Indian bread. She had one great big oven and then a middle sized oven called a family oven and then she had one little tiny one for me. And she also had my earthen bowl. And when she made her dough, at night, I made my dough just like she did, except my measurements weren't as large as hers. I'd have to show her, and say, 'is it this much' and she'd say, 'no, that's too much.' And then I'd mix it all up, and make my dough, just the same as she would. And I'd get up early in the morning, and knead it down, and start my bread again."

Agnes Dill
Isleta Pueblo

Ildefonso Pueblo girl eating pink piki bread at festival

"There are certain foods that are traditional like Navajo cake and blue corn meal, that are served nearly all the time. But the foods that are used in ceremonies are kept very sacred and are used just for certain things.

"Way back, the girl wasn't supposed to choose the husband. The mother on the boy's side would hunt for the girl, a good healthy young woman. And she had to be a good worker. They had to watch her to see if she was good. Then after she became a woman, they would have a four-day celebration. She would wear her hair long and she would wear jewelries. At the end of the fourth day, she would bake a cake. Everybody helped. The cake might be as big as a room. Then the boy's parents would go to her mother and father and ask for her.

"When a baby comes, they put the baby with the head toward the fire, which is in the middle of the hogan. And when the baby first laughs, they celebrate. They don't celebrate birthdays or anything, but the first laugh. And whoever first made the baby laugh has to furnish a basket of foods. She holds the baby and the basket of foods and friends who come around can pick what they want from the basket of foods and take it away. The reason for this is so the baby will be kind and generous to everybody. They use corn breads and cookies in the basket. The reason for the tradition is so that the child will be a kind person."

Louva Dahozy
Navajo

INDIAN FRY BREAD

2 lbs lard or 2 quarts oil
3 cups sifted flour
1 tablespoon baking powder
½ teaspoon salt
1 cup warm water

Melt lard in 5 quart deep pot. Combine flour, baking powder, and salt in a large mixing bowl. Add warm water in small amounts and knead dough until soft but not sticky. Sometimes more flour or water will be needed. Cover bowl and let stand for about 15 minutes.

Pull off large egg-sized balls of dough and roll out into rounds about ¼ inch thick. Punch hole in center of each round, piercing several times with fork, to allow dough to puff.

In a heavy skillet fry rounds in lard or other shortening until bubbles appear on dough, turn over and fry on other side until golden.

INDIAN TACO

is made by covering the fry bread with layers of fried hamburger meat, shredded lettuce, cheddar cheese, chopped onions, and diced tomatoes. Cover the top with red or green chili sauce according to taste.

ATOLE

3 cups water
1 tablespoon lard or oil
1 teaspoon salt
1 cup blue corn meal

Boil 2 cups water. Add oil and salt. Bring to rapid boil. Dissolve the blue corn meal in 1 cup water. Slowly add corn meal to boiling mixture and stir briskly until it thickens.

Note: Some flavor this with honey and believe it to be a cure for common disorders such as a stomach ache.

PUEBLO BREAD

1   package dry yeast
¼   cup warm water
2   tablespoons melted lard or
     shortening
1   teaspoon salt
4½ cups sifted flour
1   cup water

Dissolve yeast in water in a large mixing bowl. Add the melted lard, blending thoroughly.

Add flour alternately with the water in small amounts, beating well after each addition. The last amount may have to be kneaded into the dough by hand.

Shape the dough into a ball and place in a greased bowl. Brush top of dough with melted lard and cover with a tea towel. Allow dough to rise in a warm place for an hour or until doubled in size.

Punch down dough. Turn onto a lightly floured board and knead dough for 5 minutes. Divide dough into two and shape both parts into round loaves. Place loaves on a greased cookie tin and cover with a tea towel. Allow loaves to rise for 15 minutes.

Bake loaves in a preheated 400° oven for 50 minutes or until loaves are lightly browned.

Yield: 2 loaves

NAVAJO KNEEL DOWN BREAD

7 ears of fresh corn
2 tablespoons lard
1 cup water
Salt to taste

With a sharp knife scrape corn kernels from cob, reserving husks.

In a blender grind the kernels and transfer to bowl, add lard and water to make a paste.

Divide the mixture into seven parts and fill the reserved husks. Tie husks at both ends, then, gently bend husks in half and tie again.

Wrap husks in aluminum foil and bake in preheated oven at 350° for one hour or until firm to the touch. Serve.

Yield: 7 servings

SOPAPILLIAS

3 cups flour
2 teaspoons baking powder
1 teaspoon salt
3 tablespoons butter or shortening
3 eggs
¼ cup sugar
⅓ cup water, approximately
Oil for deep fat frying
Honey or ½ cup sugar mixed with 1 teaspoon cinnamon

Sift together the flour, baking powder and salt in a bowl. Cut in the butter or shortening with a pastry blender until mixture resembles coarse meal.

Beat eggs and sugar together thoroughly and add to dry ingredients with enough water to make a soft dough. Knead on a floured board until smooth and elastic, about 10 minutes. Cover with a towel and let stand for 30 minutes or longer.

Roll out to ⅛-inch thickness and cut into 3-inch squares. Fry, two to three squares at a time, in the oil (heated to 385 to 400 degrees) for 2½-3 minutes, turning to brown evenly. Drain on paper towels. Serve with honey or dip in the sugar/cinnamon mixture.

Yield: 3 dozen

TORTILLAS

4 cups blue or yellow cornmeal
2 teaspoons salt
4 teaspoons baking powder
2 tablespoons lard
Warm water or milk

Combine flour, salt, baking powder in a large mixing bowl, blending thoroughly. Work in lard thoroughly. Add water or milk gradually until dough is stiff but not sticky. Knead in bowl for 5 minutes.

Pull off a small piece of dough and roll it into a flat round of 6 inches in diameter and ⅛-inch thick.

Heat a large ungreased skillet or griddle and drop tortilla one at a time onto skillet. Brown one side and turn, brown other side. Place tortillas in a tea towel to remain warm until serving. (They will stay warm in the towel for at least 15 minutes.)

Note: White and/or wheat flour may be substituted for cornmeal.

Yield: 6-8 servings

WILD SAGE BREAD

1 package dry yeast
1 cup cottage cheese
1 egg
1 tablespoon lard or other shortening, melted
1 tablespoon sugar
2 teaspoon crushed dried wild sage
1 teaspoon salt
¼ teaspoon baking soda
¼ cup lukewarm water
2½ cups flour

Mix dry ingredients together.

Dissolve yeast in warm water.

Beat together egg and cheese until smooth. Add melted shortening and yeast.

Combine all ingredients in a large mixing bowl, adding flour mixture in small amounts and blending thoroughly after each addition. Form a stiff dough. Cover dough with a tea towel and allow to rise in a warm place for an hour or until dough has doubled in size.

After dough has doubled, punch dough down and knead for one minute. Place dough in a well-greased loaf or casserole pan. Cover and allow to rise again for 40 minutes. Bake in a preheated 350° oven for 50 minutes or until bread sounds hollow when tapped.

Yield: 1 loaf

BLUE CORN BREAD

1½ cups blue cornmeal
2 teaspoons baking powder
3 tablespoons sugar
¾ cup milk
1 large egg, beaten
3 tablespoons bacon fat
1 small can green chilies, chopped

Combine first three ingredients. Mix remaining ingredients in separate bowl.

Add liquid mix to dry ingredients and mix thoroughly.

Pour into greased baking pan and bake in preheated oven at 350° for 30 minutes or until toothpick comes out clean.

Yield: 4 servings

FRYING-PAN CORN BREAD

1½ cups flour
1½ cups blue cornmeal
6   teaspoons baking powder
1   teaspoon salt
¼   cup sugar
6   tablespoons grated cheese
¼   cup chopped sweet peppers
¼   cup chopped onion
6   tablespoons shortening or cooking
    oil
2   teaspoons ground red chili
1½ cups milk
2   eggs, lightly beaten

Sift together all the dry ingredients,
except the chili powder, in a large
mixing bowl. Add green pepper,
onion, and cheese.

In a heavy skillet, melt shortening or
heat oil and mix in chili powder. Allow
mixture to cook and add milk and
eggs. Add milk and egg mixture to dry
ingredients, blending thoroughly.

Return mixture to skillet and bake in a
preheated 400° oven for 35 minutes.
Cut in wedges and serve hot.

Yield: Eight servings

SWEET PUMPKIN BREAD

3   cups sugar
1   cup salad oil
4   eggs, beaten
2   cups canned pumpkin, mashed
2   teaspoons baking soda
3   cups flour
1   teaspoon nutmeg
1   teaspoon cinnamon
1   cup dates, chopped
1   cup nuts, chopped
¼   cup water

Mix sugar, oil, and eggs, together. Add
pumpkin, blending thoroughly.

Sift dry ingredients together, adding
water in small amounts a little at a time.
Mix in nuts and dates.

Divide mixture between 2
well-greased loaf pans. Bake in a
preheated 350° oven for 1½ hours or
until breads feel hollow when tapped.

Yield: 2 loaves

PUEBLO CORN PUDDING

5 ears of cooked fresh corn or 4 cups frozen corn kernels
2 zucchini, diced
2 small sweet green peppers, chopped finely
4 tablespoons sunflower seeds, shelled and crushed

If using fresh corn, scrape off kernels with sharp knife.

Mash all ingredients until milky or puree in a blender.

Place in a saucepan and bring to a boil. Reduce heat to low and simmer until mixture thickens.

Note: Serve hot with butter or chili sauce

Yield: 6 servings

PUEBLO PEACH CRISP

6 fresh peaches, pitted and cut into ¾-inch slices (5-6 cups)
¼ cup white sugar
¼ teaspoon salt
¾ cup flour
¾ cup brown sugar
½ cup butter

Place peaches in a shallow baking pan or casserole.

Mix white sugar and salt and sprinkle over peaches.

Combine flour and brown sugar in a mixing bowl and cut in butter until mixture is formed into small balls. Sprinkle mixture over peaches.

Bake in a preheated 375° oven for 45 minutes or until top is lightly brown and crumbly. Serve warm with whipped cream or scoop of vanilla ice cream.

Yield: 6-8 servings

LITTLE FRUIT PIES

1½ cups flour
1 teaspoon baking powder
½ teaspoon salt
6 tablespoons shortening
¼ cup water
Filling: prune, apple, or pumpkin

Combine flour, baking powder, and salt. Cut in shortening, blending until dough is the consistency of fine meal. Add water gradually until a stiff dough is formed.

Roll out dough on a lightly floured board to a ½-inch thickness. Cut dough into rounds of 4 inches in diameter. Place a heaping tablespoon of fruit filling into the center of each round. Top rounds with remaining cut rounds, pinching ends together.

Bake pies in a preheated 400° oven for about 10 minutes or until golden.

Yield: Approx. 6 servings

PUEBLO INDIAN COOKIES

2 cups butter
1½ cups sugar
2 eggs
6 cups flour, sifted
3 teaspoons anise seed, crushed
3 teaspoons baking powder
1½ teaspoons salt
1 cup Milk
Cinnamon
Sugar

Cream butter, sugar, and eggs until light and fluffy.

In another mixing bowl, mix the remaining ingredients, blending thoroughly. Add to lard or butter mixture, mixing well.

Gradually add small amounts of milk to the mixture to make a soft but stiff dough. Roll out dough on a lightly floured board and cut into cookie designs. Dip cookies into a mixture of equal amounts of cinnamon and sugar.

Place cookies on a buttered cookie sheet and bake in a preheated 350° oven for 12-15 minutes or until golden.

Yield: 6 dozen

BLUE CORN MEAL CAKES

1½ cups flour
1½ cups blue corn meal
4 teaspoons baking powder
1 teaspoon salt
1½ cups milk
¼ cup sugar
2 eggs, lightly beaten
6 tablespoons shortening or oil
4 teaspoons ground red chili

Sift together flour, blue cornmeal, baking powder, salt, and sugar.

Combine milk, eggs, shortening, and ground chili. Add to flour mixture, blending thoroughly.

Pour mixture into a greased baking pan and bake in a preheated 350° oven for 30 minutes. Serve cut in wedges.

Yield: 8 servings

NAVAJO CAKE

6 cups water
4 cups cooked blue corn meal
2 cups cooked yellow corn meal
½ cup raisins
1 cup sprouted wheat
½ cup brown sugar

Bring water to a boil in a large heavy saucepan.

Add blue cornmeal, yellow cornmeal, raisins, sprouted wheat, and brown sugar, stirring constantly over low heat. Blend until all ingredients are thoroughly mixed.

Pour mixture into a large baking pan or casserole and cover with foil. Bake in a preheated 250° oven for 4 hours or until cake is firm.

Yield: 8 servings

PIÑON CAKES

1½ cups whole wheat flour
½ cup piñon nuts, ground to meal
2 teaspoons baking powder
¾ teaspoon salt
2 tablespoons sugar
2 tablespoons lard, butter or
margarine
¼ cup water

Sift flour, nuts, salt, and baking powder together. Add shortening and sugar, mix thoroughly. Add water in small amounts to make a soft but not sticky dough.

Knead dough on a lightly floured board for 5 minutes. Place in a bowl, cover, and let stand for 15 minutes.

Pinch off egg-sized balls from dough and roll balls into round cakes of ⅛-inch thickness.

Bake in a preheated 350° oven for 10 minutes or on a griddle. Use as hot bread or serve with honey.

Yield: 10 cakes

POCKET BOOK ROLLS

2 cups flour
2 teaspoons baking powder
½ teaspoon salt
2 tablespoons shortening
⅔ cup milk

Sift flour. Add baking powder and salt to flour and sift again.

Add shortening to flour and then add milk in small amounts until a moderately stiff dough is formed.

Knead for a few minutes on a lightly floured board. Roll out dough to ¼-inch thickness. Cut dough into rounds of 4 inches diameter. Fold rounds in half. Pinch edges firmly together. Place on a baking pan, brush with melted butter, cover with a towel and allow rounds to rise for 20 minutes or until they have doubled in size.

Bake in a preheated 450° oven for about 15 minutes.

Yield: 6 servings

INDIAN BREAD PUDDING

½ cup raisins
1 cup hot water
½ loaf of sliced bread, toasted
2 eggs, beaten
¾ cup brown sugar
1 teaspoon vanilla extract
1 teaspoon cinnamon
½ cup cheddar cheese, shredded
½ cup milk

Soak raisins in hot water.

Toast the bread and allow to cool.

Add beaten eggs, brown sugar, vanilla extract and cinnamon to raisins.

Layer bread, cheese, and raisin mixture in a baking dish or casserole. Add milk.

Bake in a preheated 350° oven for 30 minutes or until all the liquid has been absorbed and pudding is firm.

Yield: 6-8 servings

TAOS PUDDING

6 cups milk
4 eggs, separated
8 tablespoons cornstarch
1 cup sugar, plus 2 tablespoons
1 tablespoon vanilla
3 tablespoons water

In a bowl mix 1 cup of sugar with the egg yolks. In a separate bowl combine cornstarch with remaining sugar.

Fold cornstarch in yolk mixture add vanilla and water and blend well.

Over low flame warm milk, add mixture stirring constantly until thickened. Cool.

Beat egg white to a peak and gently fold into cooled pudding.

Yield: 6 servings

EASTER PUDDING

4 cups sprouted wheat meal
2 cups whole wheat flour
8 cups boiling water
¾ cup sugar
¾ cup molasses
3 tablespoons butter

In a large baking dish or casserole combine wheat meal and flour and mix thoroughly. Add 7 cups boiling water to make a thick paste, cover and let stand.

Carmelize sugar. Add 1 cup boiling water and molasses, stir to make syrup.

Pour syrup over wheat mixture. Bake in a preheated 250° oven for 4 hours or until pudding is thick and dark brown. Serve with whipped cream.

Yield: 6-8 servings

DATE PUDDING

1 cup white sugar
1 cup flour
1 cup chopped dates
½ cup chopped nuts
½ cup milk
2 teaspoons baking powder
¼ teaspoon salt
2 cups water
2 cups brown sugar
1 tablespoon butter

Mix together white sugar, flour, dates, nuts, milk, baking powder, and salt. Spread mixture in a 8 x 8 inch buttered baking pan.

In a heavy saucepan, combine water, brown sugar, and butter. Bring to a boil, reduce to low heat, stirring for 2-3 minutes to make certain ingredients are well mixed. Pour liquid into baking pan.

Bake pudding in a preheated 350° oven for 45 minutes or until pudding is firm. Invert onto a plate and serve with whipped cream.

Yield: 6-8 servings

APRICOT RICE PUDDING

3 tablespoons raw rice
1 tablespoon sugar
1 quart milk
¼ teaspoon salt
¾ teaspoon cinnamon
½ cup soaked dried apricots, diced
2 eggs

Wash rice. Combine rice with all other ingredients except for the eggs.

Separate eggs. Beat egg whites until very stiff. Add beaten egg yolks to egg whites, folding in gently.

Add egg mixture to rice mixture, blending gently. Transfer mixture to a baking pan or casserole and bake in a preheated 250° oven for two hours, stirring frequently so mixture does not stick.

Yield: 6 servings

FRY BREAD PUDDING

6 pieces fry bread, split into thin halves.
1 cup sugar
1 cup water
½ cup raisins
1 teaspoon cinnamon
1 cup grated mild cheddar cheese

Caramelize sugar, add water to make syrup.

Layer fry bread alternately with raisins and cheese in a baking dish or casserole.

Pour syrup over mixture and bake in a preheated 300° oven for 20-30 minutes or until all the syrup is absorbed.

Yield: 4 servings

PUEBLO TURNOVERS

1   yeast cake
3-4 cups flour
¼   cup warm water
¾   cup milk
2   tablespoons lard or other solid
     shortening
1   tablespoon sugar
½   teaspoon salt

Filling:
dried peaches, or apricots, or apples
2 tablespoons honey

Soak dried fruit overnight in water to cover. Boil in water until tender. Chop fruit finely and add honey.

Dissolve yeast in warm water.

Mix fat, salt, sugar and milk and heat gradually until shortening is melted. Cool to lukewarm and add yeast gradually. Stir in flour to make a soft but still stiff dough.

Shape into rounds about 3-inches in diameter and ¼-inch thick.

Place a spoonful of filling on one half of each round, fold over other half of round and pinch edges firmly together.

Grease tops of round, place in a shallow, greased baking pan, cover with a cloth and let rounds double in size.

Bake in a preheated 400° oven until crusty and lightly browned.

Yield: 6 servings

LAGUNA CAKE PUDDING

1   quart milk
1½   cups corn meal
2   teaspoons powdered ginger
¾   cup molasses
½   teaspoon salt

Scald milk. Continue to simmer milk, add corn meal gradually and stir constantly until mixture thickens. Remove from heat and allow to cool.

Add ginger, molasses and salt, blending until mixture is smooth. Turn mixture into a well-greased pan and bake in a preheated 350° oven for 1½ hours.

Yield: 8 servings

PIÑON COOKIES

2 cups whole wheat flour
4 cups white flour
2 teaspoons baking powder
1 teaspoon salt
2 cups butter
1½ cups sugar
¾-1 cup water
1 cup shelled and chopped piñon
    nuts
Cinnamon
Sugar

Combine flour, baking powder, and salt. In another bowl, cream butter, and sugar until fluffy. Gradually add flour alternately with water until a stiff dough is formed. Add piñon nuts, blending thoroughly.

Roll out the dough on a lightly floured board to a ½-inch thickness. Cut into cookies with cookie cutters. Sprinkle cookies in equal amounts of cinnamon and sugar.

Bake cookies on a well-greased cookie tin in a preheated 350° oven for about 15 minutes or until golden.

Yield: Approx. 8 dozen

FEAST DAY COOKIES

2 cups sugar
2 cups lard or shortening
3 whole eggs
4½ teaspoons baking powder
1 teaspoon vanilla
6 cups flour, sifted
1 cup milk
Cinnamon
Sugar

Cream sugar and lard or shortening. Add eggs to sugar mixture, blending thoroughly. Add baking powder, vanilla, and flour, blending thoroughly. Add milk gradually until dough is stiff. Roll out dough on a lightly floured board to a ½-inch thickness. Cut into cookies with cookie cutters. Dip cookies into equal parts of cinnamon and sugar to taste.

Bake cookies on a well greased cookie pan in a preheated 350° oven for about 15 minutes or until golden.

Yield: Approx. 8 dozen